7 STEPS TO EMOTIONAL FREEDOM

7 Steps To Emotional Freedom

Jeanette Farrell

Academy of Impactful Motivation

Contents

One

—————

Foreword:

First and foremost, I would like to express my profound gratitude to you for supporting this doctrine. I am so grateful for you. You matter to me. Practicing Mindfulness has truly transformed my life. With this in mind, I hope to help transform yours. I am so grateful for everyone that believed in me and my mission to transform lives. I would like to thank God for the vision and the foundation to build upon. Next, I would like to thank my mentors: Les Brown for giving me a voice; Steve Harvey for reminding me of God's role in my vision; Stormy Wellington for encouraging me to do more and Grant Cardone for giving me the blueprint to my success. A special thank you to my beautiful family for putting up with me while I was writing this series. You are awesome and you will always have my love gratitude and honor. I am grateful to the publishers for believing in me and pushing my vision through. I am grateful for this new platform to be able to share with and help others. Positive Vibes Only People. Keep Moving Forward. Time to leave the past in the past. Let's go!

"The secret of getting ahead is getting started" – **Mark Twain**

In Loving Memory of Roger Brent Smith. May the peace of God be with you Dearest Brother who much like Mark Twain's Tom Sawyer, lived life to the fullest as a youth. Roger was taken before he could see his dreams fully manifested, I think of him as I write now, as I live now and as I breathe now. There is new purpose in my stride. No regrets. Forever in my heart, rest now Beloved Brother.

Two

Let Go !

Stop allowing the ghosts of your past to haunt your
present. Learn to Let Bad Things Go
It's easier than you think.
Emotional Freedom in 7 Little Steps
Introduction:

Too often in life, we experience troubled times, and are forced to make decisions that may not turn out as we intended. Then we may wind up being weighed down by those very decisions. Bad decisions, if not properly dealt with, can turn into a virtual tombstone. If we do not take the time out to properly acknowledge a faulty end and move on, we can end up standing still for decades on end. We then start an endless cycle of regret that leads to more regret and worse decisions in an ill-fated attempt to compensate for the regret of the prior mistakes. Do you see where I'm getting at with this? Regret leads to regret and more and more regret! This cycle should end now! Perhaps it's not an action that you regret but the lack of action. A lack of action can turn into a haunting of regret. I am here to be that virtual slap in the face. POW!!! Make It Stop! A new day is dawning for you. Read this book and take action to correct the mistakes of the past and leave them there. No more ghosts in your house. Embark with me on this journey of learning to be present. As you embark on this journey you will begin to see that the quality of your life and your relationships will significantly improve. Things will start working out for you. Trust and believe and allow this guidebook to show you the way.

Three

Jumping In

Remember this sentence "Everything is always working out for me." Repeat it several times a day like medicine.

Write it in a journal several times. Fill the page with these words. Let me come into agreement with you that everything is always working out for you. As you write, think about the everything that you want to work out. What is it that you truly want? Form a picture in your mind's eye and start writing. EVERYTHING is always working out for me. Everything IS always working out for me. Everything is ALWAYS working out for me. Everything Is always WORKING out for me. Everything is always working OUT for me. Everything is always working out FOR me. Everything is always working out for ME. EVERYTHING IS ALWAYS WORKING OUT FOR ME! Your turn.

Matthew 7:7-8 *"Ask and it will be given to you; seek and you will find; knock and the door will be opened to you. [8] For* everyone who asks receives; the one who seeks finds; and to the one who knocks, the door will be opened." **GOD**

Four

═══════════

The Truth About The Lie

Let's talk about how we got here. Are you living with regret? Have you done things in the past that you wish you'd done differently? Haven't we all? The problem isn't in the deed itself, but in being unwilling or unable to let go of your regret. Renown pastor of Elevation Church, Steven Furtick said: "Regret is taking the wisdom meant to serve you in your future and applying it to your past." If you spend too much time dwelling on things that can't be changed, you won't be able to build a better future for yourself. Use mistakes of the past as they were meant to be used, as lessons learned to change your future.

Do any of these thoughts sound familiar to you:

- How I wish I hadn't said that...
- What an unwise decision *that* was...

- If only I had spent more time with my kids...
- Why did I start this business...
- I should've never moved here...
- I should not have quit that job...
- I should not have bought that car...
- I should not have stayed in that relationship...

- Regret is a terribly sad, negative and unnecessary emotion. Even though we know we can't change the past, it still has the ability to dethrone us. It, like a magnet will draw a negative mindset leaving you in a platform of negative vibes towards everything that you think and do. Ugh, sour grapes, who wants some? You literally feel small and defeated at every turn. That kind of thinking drains your energy. You find yourself feeling tired all the time even after just waking up from a restful sleep. It's time to take your life back. Fix your crown King, Queen, the world is your kingdom for the taking. Repeat after me: "It's in the mindset not the offset."

If we don't learn how to deal with regret in positive ways, it can negatively affect the rest of our lives.

It can be extremely difficult to move on in life when we are constantly cuddled up in bed with our regret movie playing in our minds. This is why learning to let go is paramount.

"Many of life's failures are people who did not realize how close they were to success when they gave up" – **Thomas A. Edison**

Five

Reflection March 2020

Do not give in to the fear of living in the past. giving in is giving up. Don't let that be you.

Reflection March 2020

We were at work, and it was business as usual. In the middle of flu season. We had a patient who came into our unit with shortness of breath and was being treated for pneumonia. For some odd reason someone suggested we test this patient for Corona Virus and so we did, and he became our patient zero.

Pandemonium ensued after that. The staff ran scared because what we knew of this virus was that it was highly contagious and had killed thousands in China. It was no respecter of persons. It was as if the very devil himself were reincarnated in the form of this virus and wreaking havoc all over, then he had arrived at our doorstep. Mass destruction was occurring in rapid formation in its path, and it had now come to our home. Abba, I called His name freely. I drew comfort in it.

We found out about patient zero near the end our shift so the true effect for me did not take hold until afterwards. I was off for a few days after that. I remember being at home petrified about having to return to work and possibly be assigned what I thought to be a death warrant patient. I considered not returning.

I was a single parent of 6, I had an elderly mother that lived with me and hell, I just didn't feel like being the sacrifice. I prayed and prayed on these thoughts. I played the lotto; I searched up other lines of work and I asked God to speak to my heart.

Sunday rolled around and my family and I went to church. My pastor's sermon title this particular week was appropriately named "Fear Not" As he got up on the pulpit and began to speak, he laid out a picture that was as clear as the nose on my face that God was with us and would not let Corona virus touch us. I walked out of that sermon feeling like a giant slayer.

I went to work the next day ready to volunteer to take that patient. Our small minds could not comprehend at the time that very soon 100 % of our patients would be corona virus sufferers. As the numbers of our positive corona virus patients grew my prayer life and my faith grew stronger. Faith was all I had. I put that on like armor each day that I went out to do God's work and take care of the sick.

When my patients grew sicker, I prayed and cried. I held many hands in prayer on that ward. I grew bolder than my inner self was. I had to be brave and carry strength with me as I met with the eyes of fear, uncertainty and too many times ultimately death. I showered them with hope, love, and faith. I would like to think that many eyes and hearts were turned towards God in the midst of their suffering and some in their journey home.

Isaiah 41:10
New King James Version
[10] Fear not, for I *am* with you;
Be not dismayed, for I *am* your God.
I will strengthen you,

Yes, I will help you,
I will uphold you with My righteous right hand.' **GOD**

Six

The Power of Prayer

I prayed with and for everyone believer or not. They all con-sented and the ones who couldn't received about them the umbrella of my faith. Week after week I garnered renewed strength from my church community and my pastor. He was like an Angel sent to do the Lord's work. He became my real-life hero when he called upon the masses to do a prayer initiative and set up a website for us to pray without ceasing. He said God is calling us to action we must pray without ceasing. Each person signed up to pray at a particular hour so that all 24 hrs in a day was covered.

We did this every day. The goal was for someone to be praying every hour of the day to bring an end to corona virus. My hours were 5 am and 9 pm. I set an alarm on my phone and arose each morning, knelt on my knees and prayed. Each night before bed I prayed.

This was my daily prayer:

Dear God,
The God of Isaac, Abraham, and Jacob, I come to you now as your humble servant in fervent prayer and supplication. Father, ABBA, sing to me now, answer my call. I plead with you day and night. Save my nation. Rescue us from this epitome of hell that we are in. Stand with us now God. We believe in you. You and you alone can save us.

Father too many have perished. It saddens me that they perish alone God. Save us from this invisible monster. It is stealing and robbing us God. Be our comforter Jehovah Raffa be our healer Jehovah Nissi be our everything now God. Fill us with your hope and love. Have mercy on us oh God.

Touch the hearts and minds of every scientist, researcher, doctor, and technician working to find a cure for Covid 19 God. Touch the hearts and minds of every healthcare professional working to save lives oh mighty God.

Help each and every one of us to be compassionate to every-one that we encounter Lord. Help us to be patient and kind even with the families of those affected Lord. Help those in positions

of power to be more understanding and empathetic to those that are on the frontlines fighting this disease. Help them to be more willing to fill our needs dear God.

Help us to see each other and comfort each other in these difficult times. May we be able to talk about you freely where we couldn't before Lord. We honor you and give you all the glory. Please heal our patients. God only in a way that you can. Full recovery. Let them run and not be weary and boast of the great wonders that Our God performed.

Save them all God right now today, Lord. Banish this virus back to the pits of hell from whence it came.
Thank you, God, for all that you are doing and all that you will do. I look to you always. My love and reverence go to you. In Jesus name Amen, Amen, and Amen.

john 14:12 "Most assuredly, I say to you, he who believes in Me, the works that I do he will do also; and greater *works* than these he will do, because I go to My Father. [13] And whatever you ask in My name, that I will do, that the Father may be glorified in the Son. [14] If you [c]ask anything in My name, I will do *it.* "**GOD**

Seven

Oh Ye of Little Faith

I wrote, saved, and prayed this prayer twice a day for many months. I added the names of my patients and their family members each day. The list grew longer and longer. As the numbers of the fallen rose each day, I began to lose hope. The power of being chosen waned and I began feeling regret that I stayed in that losing environment.

I felt Regret that I had ever believed that prayer alone could change this thing.

There was a huge disconnect going on with me as by this time Church services had ceased in person, and I no longer felt covered. I felt exposed. I am an energy person, I fed off of energy. I needed the connection. Without it, I felt as if all of it was a lie. This was as close to atheism that I had become in my entire life.

My beliefs began to reflect in my environment. I had become a full-on pessimist. Helping others was all of who I was. I lived for it but day after day I felt like I could no longer be who I was.

The circumstances dictated that I become someone new. It was time to introduce the person in me that liked to help herself. My ship was sinking fast and a voice from within was screaming Save Yourself! I finally garnered the nerve to walk away from a job that I had once delighted in.

Hebrews 11:1
King James Version

11 Now faith is the substance of things hoped for, the evidence of things not seen. **GOD**

Eight

My Saving Grace

My Saving Grace

Fast forward eight months later. I was making more money than I had ever made in my life, but happiness was still lost. Peace was lost. Whoever said money can bring happiness was wrong. Peace is needed first. Without a peace of mind and heart, there is no joy. Joy comes from within. Created by your inner self. Joy can come to you as you are waiting in line at the food pantry. It is a free gift. Nothing or no one can buy it.

Many impulse buys are predicated on the belief of joy purchased. Purchased joy is short lived. This is why so many filthy rich people end up taking their own lives. The pursuit of joy can be relentless and futile, if you are searching externally. True everlasting joy lives within and is planted like an oak tree. Deeply rooted and outstretched to the sun.

This I now know but back then, in pursuit of joy, I pivoted again and became a travel nurse. I took my young family on the road. Somewhere between the two cities that I found myself living in months at a time, I began to realize that I needed to make a mental change. And a change of heart. It hit me that the problem was not external, it was happening on the inside of me. I made a lot of money, but nothing was working out for me.

I became a series of missed opportunities and random very expensive expenses and once I sat back and took the time to evaluate how I had ended up there, I began the root work to make a real change. I followed this systematic approach that I will teach you to decondition my mind and remove old familiar negative chatter and then reprogram my mind into clarifying, action taking, self-actuating, forward movements. That was when I finally began to live again.

"People who succeed have momentum. The more they succeed, the more they want to succeed, and the more they find a way to succeed. Similarly, when someone is failing, the tendency is to get on a downward spiral that can even become a self-fulfilling prophecy" – **Tony Robbins**

Nine

Let Your Priorities
Guide You

Step One: Let your Priorities Guide You

I started to meditate more frequently and rely on the affirming thoughts of who I wanted to be to retrain my thoughts. I began to research and study what being present was. Eckhart Tolle, Oprah Winfrey, Steve Harvey, Les Brown, Deepak Chopra, Sadhguru, they all spoke of and practiced this thing called mindfulness. I started listening to Napoleon Hill and taking notes.

"Whatever the mind can conceive and believe, it can achieve"
– Napoleon Hill.

"The only limits in our life are those we impose on ourselves."
Bob Proctor

"Accept yourself as you are. Otherwise, you will never see opportunity. You will not feel free to move toward it; you will feel you are not deserving." **Maxwell Maltz**

I stopped calling friends and family to complain about my situation and instead I allowed the words of these few mind mastery innovators to speak to my heart and mind. There were quite a few people that spoke about the actual science of your mind and being in the medical field I became intrigued and wanted to learn more. Most people that I know believe that mind science is just hocus pocus and for the crazies, but metaphysics is a very real actual science and a well-known secret among the wealthy. It's time that we all took a good, long look at it too.

The gist of what I discovered was whatever I meditate on I would attract more of. So if I continued to focus on this pain that I felt from all of the losses that I had experienced in my life the pain would be nourished and grow unto consumption. That is that the pain would be fed so well that it would build itself up in me and eventually consume me. That is the place where suicide and random acts of violence comes from.

That is the place that you nor I ever want to end up. So

instead, we will take the time out to learn how to make the pain stop. The first step is learning about energy. Metaphysics. There is energy all around us. We are made up of energy, our thoughts, meditations control the flow of the energy.

The Bible speaks of the same energy. I always loosely believed this but now I had scientific proof and I wanted to make a change. Where your focus goes the energy will flow. So,

I began the process of reprogramming like this.

I had post-it's on my bathroom mirror in the hotel room with my affirmations written on them.

My affirmatios were simply things that I wanted to believe about myself. The person that I wanted to be looking at when I looked in the mirror. I knew that I did not want someone else to tell me who I was. The world is a cynical place, and everybody is a critic. I was seeking more positive vibes. It felt good to change my beliefs about myself. To step out of the box that others placed me in. Some people look at you and all they see are those 10 things that you did wrong in your life. They want to constantly remind you of who they say that you are.

Those children that you had out of wedlock or of the time that you were almost evicted. When your fiancé left you for another woman, when you had nothing. All they will ever see in you is the negative past. They will not celebrate your wins. They choose to forget the 10000 good parts of you or your past and they hold on to the bad. Do not join them. During this transformation time keep your circle small and become your own champion. Learn to clap for yourselves.

In my book 60 Day Journey to you, I encourage you to write down your wins daily. Celebrate yourself.

I would look in the mirror and speak my affirmations daily. Honestly, some days I couldn't meet my own eyes in the mirror, I was careful to look away and focus on the words not the vision. I was so disappointed with me. I had so very many regrets. They weighed me down. I definitely had a lot of work to do. I started seeing a therapist, we concluded that I was not depressed, just shaken and that I had some healthy coping habits. Keep meditating and journaling was what she advised.

I was going through so much internal turmoil and pain and even though I was surrounded by loved ones, I felt all alone with my pain. They constantly wanted to remind me that I had no husband and all those children among other things. It felt like it was just me facing the giants. Although I had relationships that were considered to be close, I was not intimate about my true feelings with anyone. I was afraid to be. My pain felt too large for me. I didn't think that anyone else could handle it. Here is one of my journal entries, I wrote this one after I sabotaged a relationship with an emotionally intelligent man that I thought that I loved:

Reflection :

It's pouring out of me unchecked now. The good the bad the ugly all unchecked. Perhaps this is me speaking, being, living my truth. Where then is my peace, joy, and happiness. I pine away day and night for a man that barely remembers my name nor what my embers felt like while the fire that I hold for him keeps me so very warm many days and nights. SER still holds my heart and perhaps ever will. Even as I move about my will. He sits in the quiet of this new emptiness that I feel, and I marvel at how much light is found in his very remembrance. I am forever grateful for his brief but loving touch.

I think back on what drives me now in this symbiotic want of a better life for me and mines and who stands with me in my plight. As I reach around in my darkness for a hand to hold or a sure place to plant my feet, right there in my emptiness his name screams out. Oddly enough he is not a rock for me to place my feet on. But his stillness quiets my many storms and then I can climb onward. But when things around me drives me to drink and I feel like I want to crawl up a wall sideways, I meditate on God's Word and recite my affirmations like strong medicine for my hurting broken soul and I can quickly go from an empty vessel to over-flowing.

Journaling was my solace to release regret. I found my Priorities and allowed them to guide my decisions then journaling the outcomes helped me to stay in alignment with my priorities. I could reflect on the past and learn from the experiences without the pain and guilt. I found that writing down how I felt in the moment helped me to focus and to figure out how to move forward to the next step.

It's funny how passionate I felt about so very many things and people and when I read my journal entries today the memories remain, but the emotion tied to it is very much absent. What remains for me are the lessons that were learned in those moments. That is my hope for you. To be able to extract the lessons and leave behind the pain.

The good news here as well, is that there are things you can do to help prevent regret in the first place. If you should find yourself feeling regretful, there are also ways to over-come those feelings. This book will help get you to a regret-free life. True, glorious emotional freedom.

Reflection:

Years ago, as a Hospice Nurse I had the honor to serve at the bedside of a veteran's vet. I use the term twice because this 80-year young man had served the military for his entire adult life. His position and stature were so top secret that even unto his deathbed I was the only other soul in attendance.

In his last few days on earth, he relived his life to me. Only the parts that he could speak of. He told me Jeanette; I have secrets that I must take to my grave for my country but I don't regret them. My only regret is not starting a family. I was married to the military.

I understood just how much that was weighing on him now as I sat holding his hand coaching him to not fear the journey home. We had only met days before. He had no visitors in his last days, nor had he had any for the 10 years that he lived at the facility that he was in. All that he had would die with him. And I was to be the last witness to his sacrifice for his country.

His big regret of not starting a family resonated with me. In fact, in the seven years that I served as a Hospice Nurse, it was the number two most stated deathbed regret. Number one was not spending enough time with loved ones. The collection of these deathbed confessions and a series of events unfolding in my own life led to some more dynamic changes. Change can be good. Never fear change. The fear should be of remaining the same.

I literally reinvented myself into a bigger (personality wise) better me. I live life without limits and regrets. It's so freeing. I will teach you how to shed the regretful thoughts that burden your true happy, free self.

Let us reflect.

One of the best ways to make decisions you won't regret is to let your priorities guide you. Whenever you're faced with a decision, big or small, determine which option fits best with what's most important to you in the *big picture*. *Who do you see when you look in the affirmation mirror? Let that person guide you. Me? I am strong, I am confident, I am brave, I am kind, I am bold, I am endearing, I am Loving, I am loved. I am so many things. I can fill the page into overflowing. but my true question to you is who do you see and who are you showing up as?*

The option that's most closely in alignment with your

priorities, beliefs, and values will likely be the best decision for YOU.

Someone else may choose a different option, but you don't need to worry about what others think is the best – their opinion comes from their own wants and needs not yours.

If you choose what's best for *someone else, you* will be the one who regrets it. But if you choose according to your *own* priorities, regret is rarely a result. When you use this strategy to make decisions, it makes living with your decisions a whole lot easier!

Even if things don't go exactly as you planned, you can still be confident that you made the right decision for *you* based on your own needs. remember that peace of mind that we spoke of? when you relinquish control over decisions that affect your life and they turn out badly, peace of mind will be difficult to chase. Period!

I finally garnered the nerve to walk away from a job that I had once delighted in. I loved helping others. It was who I was. It took time, love, prayer, meditation, and healing for me to learn that I was much more than that. Along the way I also learned that it was ok to help myself before helping others.

"You have brains in your head. You have feet in your shoes. You can steer yourself in any direction you choose" – **Dr. Seuss**

Ten

─────────────

Learn How To Identify Your Priorities

Step Two Learning How to Identify Your Priorities

Take a moment before you move on and read these affirming thoughts out loud. I promise the big picture will start revealing itself to you soon. Repeat these words out loud or write them down as you hear yourself saying the words in your mind.

I can gently release my feelings of trying to control everything in my environment. I can go with the flow. This one was difficult for me.

I acknowledge that the only person I have complete control over is me! I cannot control the thoughts, opinions, or actions of others. However, I can control my reactions to whatever life throws my way.

I let go of my desire to control situations and I refuse to allow frustration to cloud my mind. Instead, I choose to focus on what I can do in any given situation.

Even though I cannot control everything, I am not power-less. I still have tools that help me direct my life toward achieving my goals, regardless of life's distractions.

My time management skills keep me focused and orga-nized. I allow time in my schedule for dealing with distrac-tions without losing my focus on my priorities.

Affirmations are another tool that helps guide my life to where I want to go. Regardless of what life throws at me, I can replace any negative thoughts that creep in with positive ones.

Even in hectic times, I can use breathing exercises, relax-ation techniques, and meditation to restore peace and har-mony to my soul.
I also use my optimistic outlook on life to find the positive aspect in everything.

With these tools at my disposal, I know I can go with the flow, whatever that flow might bring! I do not need to have control over anyone but myself to enjoy life with all its blessings and challenges!

Today, I choose to focus on controlling only myself and discover how joyful life can be without any desire to control others.

Self-Reflection Questions:

1.Do I feel I need to control others for my day to go smoothly?

2.How can I control my life by controlling myself?

3.What stops me from just going with the flow?

Some of these affirmations may not be for you. You will know what speaks to you when you take a good long look in the mirror. What does the best version of yourself look like? Start affirming her or him today. I am....

Reflection:

I volunteered at a mission camp one summer and as I was leaving the building for a mission one morning, I had an awakening. As I exited my sanctioned area, I looked out beyond the glass doors, and I saw what was happening around me and almost wept. It was raining steadily I saw a man. He stood close to the door but outside, beyond the call. Out in the rain he was. I watched in awe as he prepared his area. Just outside the sanctuary walls.

I watched him lay his bed. His bed was a slab of cardboard. He gently placed his valuables on top of his bed. He covered them with a rag to keep them sheltered from the rain or pilfering or both. Then as he walked away into the day he glanced back once then twice more as though to assure himself that all was well and when he was satisfied, he looked no more but walked steadily into the day by way of the beating rain.

My heart wept. I was immediately convicted. Here I was in God's House. I fought a small battle for that spot that I had claimed for my cot last night. I felt like my accommodations were too modest. In my heart I longed for home and all that came with it but that man. Oh, that man. My God That man had made his home just outside the sanctuary walls. In the outpouring of rain. I wondered just then if by him being so close to our meeting place. Perhaps some worship and works would pour out to meet him beneath the sanctuary doors that he might become convicted in the spirit and give his life over to Christ.

I wanted to meet him to if nothing else test this wonderment. I would not condemn my church for not reaching immediately beyond its walls. For I knew that condemnation was the cloak of satan. I dismissed those utterances to the back corners of my heart. Uttering a promise of my own that one day in my tomorrow years

God willing I will build a home there in that place for that man and others like him. Perhaps just four walls and a roof but something to shelter him from the rain.

I write now and the tears are held tightly at bay. I want for no man woman or child to be again without a roof and four walls to call their home. I will take up this cross if it be the will of my Father in heaven for me. Amen Amen Amen.

As convicted as I was to take action for that man, I did nothing for years to come and each time that I read that journal note, I was renewed with regret. I needed to let go.

Many times, a decision is complicated by several factors that you might consider important. Of course, each option leans a separate way, which causes confusion and uncertainty. So then, what do you do?

Follow this 3-step strategy to cut out the confusion, discover your priorities, and make decisions you can trust:

1.Reflect.

Think about what's most important to you and write them down.

- ○ Your spouse, family, and other loved ones
- ○ Your faith
- ○ Your dreams and goals
- ○ Your ethics and morals
- ○ Your health
- ○ Your work
- ○ Other things of importance to you

2.Arrange.

Put them in order with the most important items at the top.

Some of your most important priorities will change at various times in your life.

For example, if you're going to college to get a degree, completing your education may be more important than your part-time job during this time. However, when you're the sole provider for your family, your job is one of your top priorities.

3.Refer to your priority list when making choices.

Gear your decisions toward the option that provides the most advantages for the items at the top of your list whenever possible.

Go with the decision that aids the higher priority over the lower one.

- For example, when you're faced with a choice between picking up Mc Donalds on the way home from work or taking an extra 20 minutes to prepare something healthy at home, choose the healthier option. While it means a little more time to cook something healthy, your health is *always* one of your top priorities! Health is wealth!
- Things like going for a walk with your kids become easy choices because this activity satisfies two priorities: your health and spending quality time with your kids.
  You'll rarely regret making choices according to your higher priorities. On the other hand, if you should give into the feeling of the moment – like when you want junk food or would rather take a nap than spend time with your family – there may be times in the future when you regret these poor decisions.

"When you reach the end of your rope, tie a knot in it and hang on" – **Franklin D. Roosevelt**

Eleven

Live By the Golden Rule

**Step Three: Live by the Golden Rule:
Do unto others as you would have them do
unto you.**

Golden Rule

Learning to let go of fear and regret doesn't mean that magically you will begin to make all of the right choices. It simply means that your mindset will shift and once you apply the process to your decision-making wheel, you will learn to live with the choices that you made resting in the knowledge that it will be the right choice or you will learn from it.

Another effective way to prevent poor choices that lead to regret is to live by the *Golden Rule: "Do unto others as you would have them do unto you."*

Treating others with the same thoughtfulness that you'd like to receive yourself keeps you from doing or saying inconsiderate, idiotic things that you'll be sorry about later. Steep everything that you do in a healthy dose of positivity with the guidepost being will this action help or hurt someone Even if that someone is you. If you take action on that thought or idea what happens next? Would you love it or hate it if someone did those things to you?

Get in the habit of following these steps in *every-thing* you do. If you apply these lessons well the next time that you have a disagreement with someone, **you're more likely to search for a solution that benefits both of you,** rather than resorting to anger or personal attacks. When this happens, no one wins!

When you take the *Golden Rule* to heart, not only will you prevent regret, but you'll also find that **people tend to reciprocate your kindness,** making your life more enjoyable all around! No one tends to overindulge on an unsavory meal. Imagine negative thoughts and actions as being unsavory to you. You can hardly digest them. Yuk! Purge them out of your life now and watch how filled up you will get.

Twelve

Become Action Oriented

Step Four: Become Action-Oriented

Feed Your Soul

Have you ever found yourself starring into a mirror at your own reflection whispering the words of doubt over and over to yourself. Perhaps it was a raise at work that you needed to ask for or working up the nerve to ask someone out. How about this phrase Lord give me the courage to do this task? Well let me ask you, if you don't believe that you could do it why should anyone else? Try this exercise. Listen to your thoughts!

What do you hear? What words are you saying to yourself about yourself? It might sound absolutely nuts but if what you think about yourself is unflattering guess what? You started the fan club… Do this exercise with me. As you are reading this chapter, try to recall a time when you remember having positive thoughts about yourself if you must think past today then you are in deep trouble. What I am going to ask you to do next may sound silly, but it truly works. Buy a package of post its. At least a fifty pack. Buy a permanent marker too then spend about 30 minutes writing love messages to yourself. I am beautiful,

I am sophisticated, I am strong, I am intelligent, you get the idea. If there is anything positive that you believe that you are not please write that you are that. I am a Christian, so I write I am light. Keep writing until you have used the entire pack. One message per sheet. Take those sheets of life and distribute them throughout your home and office wherever you may be forced to look at it daily. Your bathroom mirror should be littered with these messages. Do not be afraid to place them in public the worse that can happen to your I am message is that someone else may read them and fall in love with themselves too.

These messages are for you to break through your objections. Try to be open minded and a little selfish at the same time. Keeping in mind that you are on a war path to win a self-incriminating case. The end result should be a stronger, bolder, confident you. Everything about a person changes when they are confident in their skin. Your walk, your smile your stance. You become a thousand times more attractive to others when you are confident.

Oftentimes, what we regret isn't so much what we did, but **what we didn't do.** Establishing an action-oriented mindset will strengthen your decision skills, too, because *your new mindset will help you make decisions that encourage action!*

Focus on making the right decision based on your priorities, then trust yourself to do what needs to be done to make your decision a reality. This level of trust will boost your confidence and enable you to achieve your goals with ease.

Here are some tips to help you develop an action-oriented mindset:

1.Avoid procrastination. When you put off doing something you *know* you should do, it'll only increase the anxiety and tension in the hours leading up to the inevitable deadline. You will regret procrastinating unless you make up your mind to handle your tasks appropriately.

- If you're putting off telling someone something, just take a deep breath and begin. If you start the conversation with pleasantries, it may help you ease into what you have to say.
- If you're procrastinating on a project, just getting started is often the only thing that holds you back. ***Start with something easy so you can build the momentum you need to move forward, faster than ever.***
- If you're not taking action because a task is too difficult, divide the task into small, easily achievable mini-goals. Once you do, you'll have a reasonable plan and you'll be less likely to get overwhelmed.

2.Plan your work and work your plan. Keep a planner and make a daily to-do list. Refer to your list often and cross out your tasks as you complete them so you can see yourself making progress all day long.

- Make your schedule flexible enough to give yourself time to handle unexpected distractions. Practice immediately taking care of the things that come up and then getting quickly back to your list.

3.Seek solutions to your challenges. So often we let an obstacle in our path stop us from pursuing the life we desire, only to regret it later.

- ***With an action-oriented mindset, challenges are only bumps in the road.*** When a challenge arises, immediately start looking for viable ways around it, then take action to continue toward your goal.

"I am not a product of my circumstances. I am a product of my decisions" – **Stephen Covey**

Thirteen

Take Advantage of Opportunities

Step Five: Take Advantage of Opportunities

Are you always "out" when opportunity comes knocking? Learning to recognize good opportunities and taking advantage of them right away can also prevent regret. How many times have you berated yourself for missing a window of opportunity? How many times did you allow fear to paralyze you into not taking action.

Before I discovered mindfulness, I was guilty of this. I frequently allowed fear to place me in a confused state where I took no action. No action meant no growth. I was stagnated by my own fear. Through meditative mindset and reflection,

I realized that fear had no place in a decision-making tree. It very often killed the tree.

One of the best – and simplest – ways to help yourself recognize valuable new ideas is to **keep an open mind.** Listen to other people's ideas and then apply them to your own situation. Ask yourself if there's a way you can use this idea to bring you closer to your goals or make your life better.

Just recognizing the opportunity, however, is not enough. Be sure to use your new action-oriented mindset to take *immediate* action. If you spend too long simply thinking about it, your window is likely to close. **Carpe Diem!** Seize the day!

"Go the extra mile, there's no-one on it" – **Grant Cardone**

Fourteen

Make Good Memories

Step Six: Make Good Memories

Being intentional. What does that mean? Live your life with purpose. It means that you **choose a life of joy, then actively pursue that life.** Spend your time making the memories that you *want* to have!

Would you rather have memories of work, boredom and wasting away your life – or joyful memories of cherished time with your spouse, friends or family? Would you rather fill your mind with memories from a Netflix binge or real-life pursuits of your dreams? Always remember that joy is intentional!

You can choose joy any day of your life. If you have no friends begin to live out your passions and the friends will come. Book a sip and paint session or a morning hike. Join a book club or your local meetup group. Get on social media and join a travel group. 0Just remain open to new friendships when they do arrive.

Surely no one has ever gone to their grave wishing that they had spent *more* time working or watching TV! These are simply *not* the things that matter the most when you look back on your life.

The secret to avoiding holding on to regret is to do the things that matters the most to you.

Reflection:

I was in the proofing stage of writing this book when tragedy struck twice in my home. The first tragedy, my daughter's plight, I will share in another book likely entitled Atrium. the second, is the plight of my brother Roger. My brother checked in to the hospital by way of EMS for a low blood sugar of 28. The hospital that I learned later the locals referred to as Killendale hospital murdered my brother. my sisters and I all in the medical field spent 10 days and nights by his side as he lay dying on a ventilator. The feelings of hopelessness and helplessness were endless. The first time that he died after the hospital neglected to check critical lab work and treat fatal heart rhythms his brain died in those 40 minutes. We prayed him back to life. I believe that God brought him back to give our hearts time to accept what was to be.

I prayed and meditated night and day. I sat like Buddha on the nasty ICU floor in meditation for my soul. I could not lose myself. Nothing made sense. My beloved brother lay dying from something that was curable if someone cared to do their job. If I were his nurse or my sister, he would be alive today. The thoughts went on in that manner. As I arose one day from meditation, I felt an awakening. I was experiencing deep regret. I felt like a hypocrite. I just wrote an entire book on this. I sat down next to my brother and pulled up my proof and began to read the manuscript to him. By the end of the reading, I had reaffirmed that this book was to be released. I once again believed in the power of letting go and let my affirming thoughts guide me. My brother was leaving us, but he left us with a beautiful son and daughter that we rededicated to. Life, our life goes on.

My brother was laid to rest in a beautiful homegoing ceremony. I found so many things to be grateful for. mostly I was grateful to have the support of my family. In those moments I was grateful for each of my children and grandchildren. for every niece, nephew, aunt and uncle. Every human touch and word.

My brother's passing took some light, but it did not break

me. I stand firm in my beliefs of moving past regret into victory. I am grateful for this book and others like it.

What about you? What do you want to do in your life? Do you want to travel? Be a stay-at-home mom or Dad? Start your own business? Then do what it takes to bring in the extra income to pay for it! Do you want to be multi-lingual? Then start learning another language *today!*

In other words, **take action to create the life you want. Look for my 60-day Journey to You Accountability Journal on Amazon. Do** not spend your time bemoaning your current situation and wishing for more. Do something *every day* to bring the life you desire into your present and exhibit the qualities you desire. Sooner than you realize, your dreams will become your reality, and you'll have thoroughly enjoyed the journey, too!

"We are what we repeatedly do. Excellence, then, is not an act, but a habit" – **Aristotle**

Fifteen

—————————

Eliminating Past Regrets

Step Seven: Eliminating Past Regrets
Reflections 2020

I should not have stayed in that relationship...

The beginning...

Lions and Bears have nothing on you. You walk as though one having all authority. You sway not. Your voice it speaks as though you hold the entire worlds knowledge-base. You eyes they are everywhere searching scanning you seem to be on at all times. I wondered briefly if I were a subject to be studied.

Quickly I dismissed the thought. You are an answered call. Hello You. Safe at last Seen at last Loved at last. An answered call to my everything. I can close my eyes with you.

When you harbor resentment about the past, it only hurts you. Nothing good comes from regret or the negative emotions that go along with it.

Reflection: The end

There is so much anger inside of me at times it feels like rage. Rage and anger at myself for always being a victim. I feel like throwing things at the wall and smashing things then at a few seconds pause I realize that it would only make me feel worst because I bought those things, my cellphone, my coffee mug, my China plate. I pay for this home. If I gave in to my inner beast, the hole that I have dug for myself would only get bigger.

The rage that I feel now is not my own in fact it was borrowed or given to me by happenstance. I feel the overwhelming desire to punch my fists through the wall now. Something I have never pondered on or even remotely had a desire to do ever in my life. But the Bible says that when a man and woman come together the two shall become one and just because I have sinned and came together with man not as husband and wife but as a woman in sexual need and a man in sexual need the principle of God remained intact. He gave to me and took of me.

This rage that I feel is of him this I know. Id like to give it back. Or shed it completely. Instead, I wonder what he took from me. I must guess as we are not speaking now. He has cut me off coldly from all communication. Strange how a man seemingly so compassionate and loving can be so bold about his darkness. My children young and old ask for him. My mother, my brother, and sisters, they all ask for him.

I cry not and comfort myself in knowing that he never cared at all for any of them or me. He Jested and played a role from the start and that is how he could boldly declare this new callous nature because it was his true self. Even armed with this new knowledge I cannot put his sweet children out of my mind. From the young to the old. Although they may have played along their true nature stained me and I long to see them. I seem to be cursed with longing.

The emptiness and loneliness that I feel seems all consuming on holidays like this. No one ever shows up for me. I know that she watches weighs and measures each moment and relishes when I am *wanting. Loneliness, her bosoms just won't leave me alone. It makes these bitter moments even harder to endure. Why my doorsteps seem so treacherous and filled with despair on these days.*

I allow people to take from me because it feels so good to give but human nature says that they will take all that you are willing to give and not have a need or desire to give anything if you allow it. That is how and when you end up with pain, bitterness and in the company of lonely on a great day like Mother's Day. Tears come too easily now. There was a time when my rain would fall only once a month to coincide with the ebb and flow of my circadian rhythm.

Even as I try to quiet my heart with alcohol. I tried to fill my mind with the task of being Mommy to my little ones and watching them go about the business of play which usually brings me untethered joy but today. Joy was elusive. my true mind hovered nearby wrapped up in a man that I never should have looked twice at much less given my heart to. He seemingly purposely shredded my pride and broke my heart in two. As though that was not enough hurt to inflict, he put the broken pieces of my heart up on display for my enemies to relish at. My family had a front row seat to my theatric demise.

I am so completely overcome. Perhaps another drink of alcohol might numb this pain. It's so sore this spot where my heart once was. I rub it and will it to return restored, but it disobeys even me.

This unruly heart of mine. So, I drank. One day in one attempt to forget this pain that I am in. I wanted to sleep for days then wake up and not remember that hurt people hurt people, and someone hurt this man so deeply that he did not bat an eyelash at hurting me so completely.

I HAVE SUFFERRED LOSS IN MY LIFE. Seemingly endless great loss. Tangible and intangible losses. This is not new to me. This is why my face can be filled with mirth and grace in the face of this fleeting loss. I have suffered many a loss. I have grieved long and over long. I have suffered loss disgracefully and suffered loss with ease.

I have become an expert is loss suffering. I could probably teach on the matter. And so, this is how I stand, and I walk, and I play and stay in the face of my adversities and adversaries I can do all things as Christ has strengthened me. Each night when I get into the shower and the rain comes the story in my heart changes a little. I thank Elizabeth Kubler Ross for helping me to recognize my pattern. I was in denial for quite a while.

Calling and texting as though nothing had changed. I couldn't believe that I was dropped like that for what seemed to be no reason at all. Then I was angry at him and me and finally God. I was angry at God for giving me everything that I thought I wanted in a man and then abruptly taken it and him away. I stopped reading The Word and walking a certain way. I bargained with God more than a few times. Before finally arriving at acceptance and moving on.

At times however my mind wanders back to remembrance, and I am transplanted back into the time and space when he captured my very breath just by being near. I couldn't meet his gaze because it befuddled my brain and rendered me incapacitated to breathe. Looking back on things now I am thankful that I could breathe again. I vow to never again engage with a breath sucker. I might not live through another attack like that one.

Ephesians 4
New International Version

19 Having lost all sensitivity, they have given themselves over to sensuality so as to indulge in every kind of impurity, and they are full of greed.

20 That, however, is not the way of life you learned 21 when you heard about Christ and were taught in him in accordance with the truth that is in Jesus. 22 You were taught, with regard to your former way of life, to put off your old self, which is being corrupted by its deceitful desires; 23 to be made new in the attitude of your minds; 24 and to put on the new self, created to be like God in true righteousness and holiness. **GOD**

Sixteen

Self-Reflection Questions:

Changing my perspective changed my life. Infact, having a new perspective saved my life. I am so much more today because of my new mindset. I feel empowered to do more have more and be more. Fear is no longer my crippling enemy. I laugh at it now. When you know who you are, no one can tell you anything differently and you fall for it. I wish a breath sucker would... I am so grateful that I am forever changed.

I boldly go where I need to go. There is a fire inside me that is blazing a trail of forward-facing actions. I am unapologetically me. I fully embrace the lessons that I have learned from the past and I am grateful for them, and I am thankful for the opportunities that I have in my tomorrows. Some may refer to this phenomenon as favor. I walk in it now but only because I was brave enough to let go of the past.

A life free from regret is a joyful life indeed! Release the need to control every single outcome. Trust the process. Remember that you are winning or learning never losing.

Strive to use these strategies and techniques to keep regret from raising its ugly head in your path so you can enjoy your journey of life. *It's going to be a wild and wonderful ride!*

More Self-Reflection Questions:

1.How often do I incorporate breathing and meditation in my work day?

2.What other benefits does meditation offer to me?

3.How do I approach asking for clarification when the other person is impatient?

4.What activities can I engage in to enhance the value of meditation?

5.How do I realign with my belief system after an emotionally challenging day?

6.In what ways can I incorporate meditation throughout the course of the day?

"It does not matter how slowly you go as long as you do not stop" – **Confucius**

Seventeen

Enter Mindfulness

Enter mindfulness.

When you harbor resentment about the past, it only hurts you. Nothing good comes from regret or the negative emotions that go along with it.

I counteract confusion with deep breathing and meditation.

There are times when I feel unsure about things, but I avoid allowing it to overwhelm me.

Centering my mind offers clarity. Taking deep breaths gives me the chance to let go of the negative emotions that are frustrating me. I return to a calm state where I can think clearly.

Having that clarity allows me to objectively think things through. I weigh the various angles and come up with a reasonable perspective.

When I am unsure about someone's sincerity, I think through all that I know about them. Calmly weighing the data allows me to formulate an informed opinion.

Meditation is the key to introducing impartiality to my assessment process.

When I am confused at work, instead of feeling stressed and uneasy about delivering the incorrect result, I take a few moments to clear my head. Deep breathing rids my mind of anything that stands in the way of my concentration. It keeps me focused on the task at hand.

I know that my ability to decipher things and make sound decisions comes from having a settled mind and spirit.

Today, clarity guides each task that I undertake and each decision that I make. My commitment to breathing and meditation is an important element of thinking clearly. I know that when my mind is clear, I am able to hear the intended message and act on it.

Here are some life hacks that can help you overcome any lingering feelings of regret:

1. **Let bygones be bygones.** Things that happened in the past cannot be changed, no matter how hard we try, or how much time we spend wishing that they had happened differently. If there is a way to make amends, do it, then move on with your life. Focus on your present, look forward to your future, and leave the past in the past.

2. **Live in the moment.** When you live in the moment, you are fully focused on the *now*. You feel the pleasures, sensations, and joys of *this* moment and appreciate all of them. The more you practice this technique, the more you can tune out everything and embrace this moment. Gratitude is the attitude. *Your days are a parade of moments, so you should fully live each one of them, one at a time.*

3. **Use affirmations.** Affirmations can help you change your mindset from feeling sad about the past to accepting it so you can live a more joyful life. They're positive statements that you can repeat to yourself every time a regretful thought presents itself.

Here are some other useful examples of affirmations:

- I let go of my regret to make room for joy.
- I am happy with who I am now and I look forward to a joyous future.
- I live each day with gratitude for this precious gift of life.

4. Meditate. Meditation helps you envision your life without regret. When meditating, feel the good feelings of a care-free life. Breathe in freshness and light then breathe out regret. See the negative feelings dissipate in the clear air around you – gone forever, never to return!

Meditation helps me to set intentions for each day.

Being present in each moment allows me to have days that are fulfilling. Conscious involvement in each thing that I do encourages positive decision making. Meditation, helps me to set my intentions for the day ahead, my centering thought is always results driven. For example: Today I will help twenty five patients or today I will make two coworkers smile. When I set intentions, I am more likely to attain them.

Each morning gives me a chance to define my purpose in life. The quiet time when I wake up helps me to formulate a plan for making the most of my time.

Meditation allows me to connect to my inner beliefs. Having that connection reminds me to focus on what I truly value. I live according to what I believe is wholesome and just.

When I look within, I consider the impact that my actions have on my circle of influence. My focus is on being a positive influence for those people.

As I meditate, I realign myself with that focus and commit to living positively for the day. I encourage my subordinates at work and extend a helping hand to those who are less fortunate.

Quiet time at the end of each day also helps me to re-center myself. Reflection allows me to identify shortcomings and develop a plan of action to overcome them.

Today, I acknowledge that there is significant value in meditation. Being able to focus on my inner being is helpful in allowing me to experience rewarding days.

"If you don't like something, change it. If you can't change it, change your attitude." – **Mary Angelou**

Eighteen

Worksheet

WORKSHEET

SELF-REFLECTION WORKSHEET

Do you have feelings of regret that you'd like to release from your mind? This worksheet will help you create a custom plan to overcome the negative emotions associated with regret.

For each of your regrets, reflect on the questions to work through your feelings.

1. List your regrets.

2. Why do you regret it?

3. How is it affecting your present life?

4. What can you do *today* to improve the current situation?

5. How will you feel when you've released your regrets?

6. Create some affirmations that encourage you to think positively when you're reminded of your regrets.

TIP: These affirmations should be positive, personal (use the word "I"), and in the present tense, as if you already possess this ideal.

7. Envision yourself without this regret. Include a description of you physically, mentally, and emotionally letting go. *How does it feel?* Make this meditation detailed and clear. Envision this meditation every day and feel the relief.

8. How can you begin to *live in the moment* during your everyday routine? Implement these solutions today.

EXAMPLES: Begin your day with a morning walk to clear your mind and enjoy nature. Fully experience the beauty of the dawn or sunset. Start a gratitude journal.

Resources

Need Support Now?

- If you or someone you know is struggling or in crisis, help is available. Call or text 988 or chat 988lifeline.org
- Disaster Distress Helpline: CALL or TEXT 1-800-985-5990 (press 2 for Spanish)

Abuse/Assault/Violence

- National Domestic Violence Hotline: 1-800-799-7233 or text LOVEIS to 22522
- National Child Abuse Hotline: 1-800-4AChild (1-800-422-4453) or text 1-800-422-4453
- National Sexual Assault Hotline: 1-800-656-HOPE (4673) or Online Chat

LGBTQ+

- Trans Lifeline: 1-877-565-8860 (para español presiona el 2)

- The Trevor Project's TrevorLifeline: 1-866-488-7386

Older Adults

- The Eldercare Locator: 1-800-677-1116 – TTY Instructions
- Alzheimer's Association Helpline: 1-800-272-3900 (para español presiona el 2)

Veterans/Active-duty Military

- Veteran's Crisis Line: 988, then select 1, or Crisis Chat or text: 838255

I AM GRATEFUL

I am so Grateful for you. You matter to me, and I am eternally grateful for you. Always be Grateful. Be Blessed, Be Well and Keep Moving Forward Friend. Now tell me who do you see when you look in the mirror?